One Wet Welly

First published 2005
Evans Brothers Limited
2A Portman Mansions
Chiltern St
London W1U 6NR

British Library Cataloguing in Publication Data
Matthews, Gill
      One Wet Welly. – (Twisters)
      1. Children's stories – Pictorial works
      I. Title
      823.9'2 [J]

ISBN 0237529289
13-digit ISBN (from 1 January 2007) 9780237529284

Printed in China by WKT Company Limited

Series Editor: Nick Turpin
Design: Robert Walster
Production: Jenny Mulvanny
Series Consultant: Gill Matthews

One Wet Welly

Gill Matthews
and Belinda Worsley

Evans

Sam and Ben went for a walk.

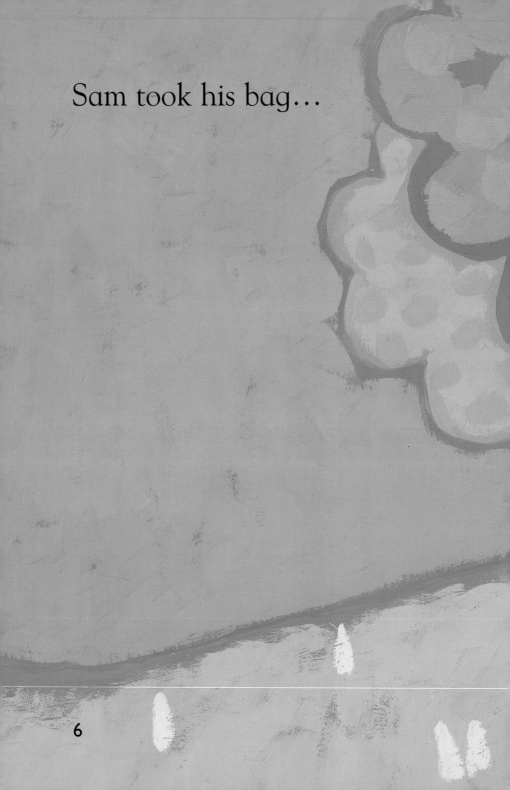

Sam took his bag…

…and Ben did, too.
They found…

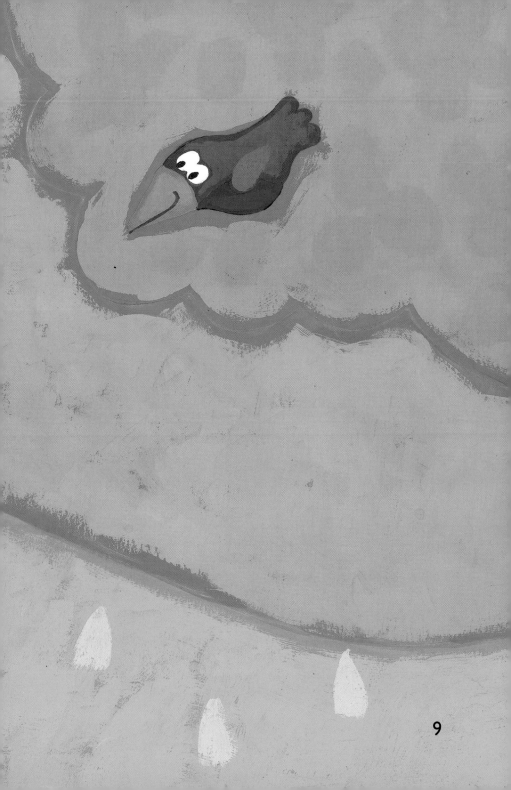

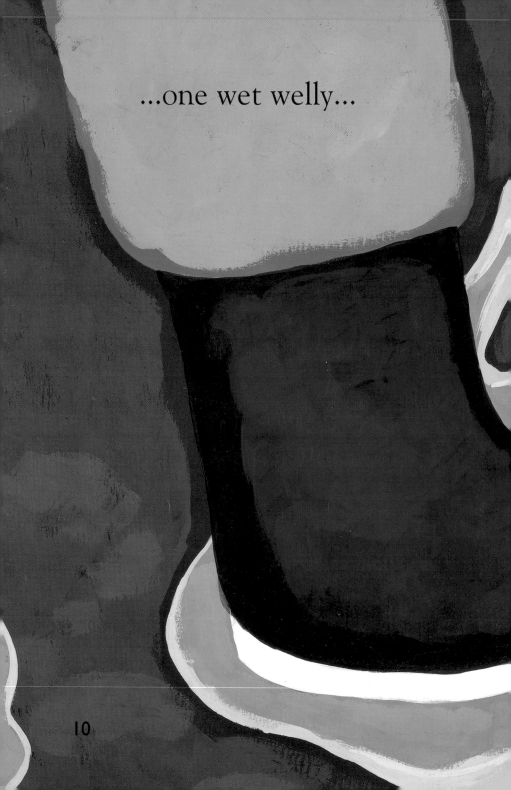

...one wet welly...

...two tiny tadpoles...

...three thorny thistles...

...four fat frogs...

...five fine flowers...

19

...six smooth stones...

...seven shiny snails...

...eight amazing apples...

...nine knobbly
nuts and...

27

...ten tired toes!

Now elevenses!

Why not try reading another Twisters book?

Not-so-silly Sausage by Stella Gurney and Liz Million
ISBN 0 237 52875 4

Nick's Birthday by Jane Oliver and Silvia Raga
ISBN 0 237 52896 7

Out Went Sam by Nick Turpin and Barbara Nascimbeni
ISBN 0 237 52894 0

Yummy Scrummy by Paul Harrison and Belinda Worsley
ISBN 0 237 52876 2

Squelch! by Kay Woodward and Stefania Colnaghi
ISBN 0 237 52895 9

Sally Sails the Seas by Stella Gurney and Belinda Worsley
ISBN 0 237 52893 2

Billy on the Ball by Paul Harrison and Silvia Raga
ISBN 0 237 52926 2

Countdown by Kay Woodward and Ofra Amit
ISBN 0 237 52927 0

One Wet Welly by Gill Matthews and Belinda Worsley
ISBN 0 237 52928 9

Sand Dragon by Su Swallow and Silvia Raga
ISBN 0 237 52929 7

Cave-baby and the Mammoth by Vivian French and Lisa Williams
ISBN 0 237 52931 9

Albert Liked Ladders by Su Swallow and Barbara Nascimbeni
ISBN 0 237 52930 0